Piano Step by Step

A Series for Young and Perennially Young Pianists

Performance Pieces · Dances · Studies · Pieces for Piano Duet

An Introduction to Style

Each volume is arranged progressively ranging from easy to medium

Eine Reihe für junge und ewig junge Pianisten

Vortragsstücke · Tänze · Etüden · Vierhändiges Spiel

Einführung in den Stil

Jeder Band ist progressiv geordnet von leicht zu mittelschwer

Une série pour jeunes et éternellement jeunes pianistes

Pièces d'exécution · Danses · Etudes · Jeu à quatre mains

Initiation au style

Chaque volume est ordonné progressivement du facile au moyen difficile

Editor of the series

Herausgeberin der Reihe

Rédactrice de la serie

Ágnes Lakos

Könemann Music Budapest

Ludwig van Beethoven
(1770–1827)

47 Piano Pieces

Compiled and provided with fingering by
Ausgewählt und mit Fingersatz versehen von
Choisis et doigtés par

Ágnes Lakos

Könemann Music Budapest
K 243

INDEX

Beethoven

Beethoven's Lifelong Companion: The Piano

Of the three greatest Viennese Classical composers (Haydn, Mozart and Beethoven), Piano meant the most to Beethoven. Haydn never intended to embark on a career as a pianist; Mozart was a phenomenon when it came to piano playing – his skill was unparalleled – but he only showed real interest in the instrument when he wanted to use it for colour either as a composer or as a brilliant performer. For both Haydn and Mozart the piano played only a minor role in the composition process, as they composed at their desks (Mozart preferred to compose in his head without external aid). But Beethoven could neither work nor live without his piano. He extemporised at the keyboard for hours before he actually set any of his musical ideas down on paper. For him, the piano was a catalyst for his outbursts of emotion, the keys lending aural expression to his soul. He hated the neighbours eavesdropping when he improvised and experimented. Being alone and playing the piano was for Beethoven a blend of prayer, confession and meditation. He was a very lonely man who, from the age of 26, was hounded by hearing difficulties which in the space of a few years left him completely deaf, an inconceivable catastrophe for a man who in his youth had been a promising virtuoso. It is hard to imagine this Beethoven, the darling of the audience, who after his "charming" performance bowed time and again to the ecstatic public, blowing kisses to the ladies present. Yet this is how his career started in his home town of Bonn. Pushed by his father, the child prodigy was mercilessly trained for the stage. When his first composition for the piano was published, the cover proclaimed him two years younger than he actually was. When he moved to Vienna at the age of 20 he tried to win over the elegant and well-to-do of the imperial city with his piano playing. He wore a green tail coat, took dancing and riding lessons and played the dandy. Sadly, fate was against him, and the hopeful young musician gradually become more isolated from the outside world. He was left alone with his piano.

Beethoven's Pianistic Style

A recording of Beethoven playing the piano would be of priceless value. Unfortunately this is beyond the bounds of possibility, for Beethoven preceded Edison by several decades. Yet various descriptions of his performance have been left to us, recounting how the notes raged and threatened at his fingertips or sparkled like stars in the descant range of the piano. His compositions tell us much more. They show us that Beethoven was a master of contrast. He loved the extreme registers, wrote incredibly long trills and unexpected rests, and often engaged the left and right hands in musical dialogue. His pianistic style changed over the years. He was influenced by Haydn and Mozart in his youth; around 1800 he presented his new, individual style with sweeping confidence and towards the end of his life he notated sounds which were not only daring and strange, but which his immediate successors were frightened to imitate, as if they were from another planet.

K 243

Beethoven's Works for Piano

Beethoven wrote an incredible number of pieces for the piano. His 32 sonatas alone have presented generations of pianists with a lifetime challenge. In them Beethoven consolidated everything he knew about keyboard music since J. S. Bach with encyclopaedic completeness. The sonatas are Beethoven's musical diary; he wrote the first one when he was only 13 and the last one five years before he died. There is another pianistic form which accompanied him throughout his life: the variation. His variations are a testimony to the most astonishing of the composer's skills, namely the art of improvisation. It is highly characteristic that the first and the last major works Beethoven composed for the piano were in variation form. He also wrote 5 piano concertos between 1795 and 1809 and a multitude of chamber works which feature the piano in a leading role (the violin and cello sonatas and piano trios). Beethoven's works are curiously logical in their chronology; the compositions for piano are not only of extreme importance, but also seem to mark the various stages in Beethoven's life. Beethoven always used music for the piano to prepare and herald a change in compositional direction. After he had opened up new avenues for himself on the piano, he then penned his impressive symphonies (9 in total, from 1800–1824) and the string quartets, a condensed, musical summary of his achievements (No.s 1–6, Op. 18, 1798–1800; No.s 7–9, the *Rasuomovsky Quartets*, Op. 59, 1806; No. 10 in Eb, Op. 74, 1809 and No. 11 in Fm, Op. 95, 1810; and the 5 late quartets No.s 12–16, including the *Große Fuge*, 1823–1826). This periodicity reveals that right from the start Beethoven had conceived his musical oeuvre as a grand whole, as his life's work. In this cosmos of sound even the smallest contributions to his music for the piano, the various dances and bagatelles (including the popular *Für Elise*, originally a bagatelle), are not without their place and significance.

Beethoven

Beethovens Lebensgefährte: Das Klavier

Von den drei großen Wiener Klassikern (Haydn, Mozart, Beethoven) war Beethoven derjenige, für den das Klavier den größten Stellenwert besaß. Haydn hatte nie den Ehrgeiz, als Pianist eine Karriere zu machen, Mozart war zwar ein Phänomen auch auf dem Klavier und war als Virtuose angesehen, aber das Instrument beschäftigte ihn nur, wenn er das Klavier als Klangmedium für seine Kompositionen und Auftritte benötigte. Im Prozeß des Komponierens spielte das Klavier bei Haydn und Mozart eine geringere Rolle, sie komponierten am Schreibtisch (Mozart sogar am liebsten im Kopf). Beethoven dagegen war sehr stark auf das Klavier fixiert. Er war als Improvisator berühmt, der stundenlang "fantasieren" konnte. Hierbei wurde das Klavier für ihn zum Katalysator seines extrovertierten Charakters, der ihm half, seinen Gefühlen tönende Form zu geben. Er haßte es, beim Fantasieren belauscht zu werden. Das einsame Klavierspiel war für ihn Meditation und Bekenntnis zugleich.

Beethoven hatte einen komplexen und oftmals schwierigen Charakter, der ihm den Umgang mit seinen Zeitgenossen erschwerte. Seit dem Alter von etwa 30 Jahren litt er an einer Erkrankung des Gehörs, die in seinen späteren Jahren zur völligen Taubheit führte. Für einen Musiker, der in seinen ersten Wiener Jahren als einer der größten Pianisten überhaupt galt, eine Katastrophe.

Sich Beethoven als Publikumsliebling vor-zustellen, der sich nach seinem bezaubernden Klavier-spiel von den Zuhörern verbeugt und Küsse für die Damen ins Publikum wirft, fällt schwer. Dennoch begann er seine Laufbahn in Bonn auf diese Weise. Als von seinem Vater, einem Tenor der Bonner Hofkapelle, forciertes Wunderkind wurde er für das Podium trainiert. Bei seiner ersten im Druck erschienenen Klavierkomposition wurde Beethoven auf dem Titelblatt um zwei Jahre jünger gemacht. Als er knapp zweiundzwanzigjährig nach Wien umsiedelte, wollte er vor allem mit seinem Klavierspiel die elegante Gesellschaft der Kaiserstadt erobern. Er trug einen grünen Frack, nahm Tanz- und Reitstunden. Aber die Krankheit kam dazwischen, und der so selbstsichere junge Musiker wurde allmählich von der Außenwelt isoliert. Er blieb allein mit seinem Klavier.

Beethovens Klavierstil

Für eine Tonaufnahme von Beethovens Klavierspiel würde die Musikwelt sicher jeden Preis bezahlen. Doch bleiben uns nur einige überlieferte Beschreibungen, aus denen wir seine Künste erahnen können: Wie er mit großer Ausdruckskraft die Bässe drohen und stürmen und den Diskant strahlen ließ. Und natürlich bleiben uns seine Noten, die viel mehr als jede wörtliche Beschreibung vermitteln. Sie zeigen, daß Beethoven ein Meister der Kontraste war. Er liebte die extremen Register, konnte unglaublich lange Triller und sogar drei zur selben Zeit fordern, fügte unerwartete Pausen ein und ließ oft die rechte und linke Hand des Pianisten dialogisieren. Sein Klavierstil änderte sich im Laufe der Zeit. In seiner Jugend war er von Mozart und Haydn beeinflußt, um 1800 präsentierte er mit großem Selbstbewußtsein einen ganz individuellen und progressiven Stil, und am Abend seines Lebens stieß er in kühne Klangwelten vor, die von seinen Zeitgenossen kaum verstanden werden konnten und für Jahrzehnte unerreicht blieben.

Beethovens Klavierwerk

Beethovens Klavierschaffen ist in Umfang und Bedeutung gewaltig. Seine 32 Klaviersonaten bildeten für Generationen von Pianisten bis heute das Zentrum ihrer Arbeit. Der strengen, kontrapunktischen Klaviermusik Bachs setzt Beethoven einen dramatischen und leidenschaftlichen Stil entgegen, der dennoch alle Errungenschaften der Klaviermusik aufgriff und weiterführte. Die Sonaten vor allem bilden geradezu ein musikalisches Tagebuch Beethovens: Seine ersten Sonaten schrieb er im Alter von 13 Jahren für den Kurfürsten in Bonn (WoO 47), die letzte fünf Jahre vor seinem Tod (op. 111). Aber auch eine andere Klaviergattung begleitete Beethoven sein Leben lang, die Variation. In den zahlreichen Variationszyklen ist seine erstaunliche Fähigkeit zur Improvisation festgehalten. Es ist bezeichnend, daß sein erstes und letztes großes Klavierwerk Variationen sind. Zur solistischen Klaviermusik treten selbstverständlich die fünf Konzerte für Klavier und Orchester (1795–1809) und eine große Anzahl von Kammermusikwerken, in denen das Klavier führende Rolle spielt (vor allem die Violin- und Cellosonaten und Klaviertrios).

Beethovens Schaffen zeigt einen merkwürdig logischen Aufbau, in dem die Kompositionen für Klavier nicht nur eine äußerst wichtige, sondern eine von Lebensabschnitt zu Lebensabschnitt wieder-kehrende Rolle spielen. Beethoven hat eine neue stilistische Orientierung stets mit Klaviermusik vorbereitet und ausprobiert. Nachdem er auf dem Klavier im eher intimen Rahmen für sich den neuen Weg gefunden hatte, übertrug er ihn auf repräsentative Werke, etwa die Symphonien, von denen er zwischen 1800 und 1824 insgesamt 9 komponierte. Dies betrifft aber auch die Streichquartette, die seine Kompositionskunst als anspruchsvollste Gattung der Zeit überhaupt in komprimierter Form zeigen. Beethoven komponierte den ersten Zyklus mit sechs Quartetten op. 18 im Jahre 1800, dann folgten 1806 drei Quartette op. 59, die nach dem russischen Fürsten Rasumowsky benannt sind. 1809 und 1810 komponierte er 2 Quartette: op. 74 "Harfenquartett" und op. 95 "Quartetto serioso". Als seine letzten großen Kompositionen vollendete er die berühmten fünf späten Streichquartette opp. 127, 130, 131, 132, 135 sowie die "Große Fuge" für Streichquartett op. 133 in den Jahren 1823 bis 1826. Diese Periodizität läßt auf eine tiefergehende Konzeption von Beethovens Lebenswerk schließen. In ihr finden auch kleine Beiträge der Klaviermusik, Tänze, Bagatellen, Klavierstücke (darunter das beliebte Albumblatt "Für Elise"), ihren Platz.

Beethoven

Le compagnon de Beethoven : le piano

Des trois grands classiques viennois (Haydn, Mozart, Beethoven), ce fut Beethoven qui accorda le plus d'importance au piano. Haydn n'eut jamais l'ambition de faire une carrière de pianiste, Mozart était également un phénomène au clavier, il jouait de manière incomparable, mais qu'il fût dans le rôle du compositeur ou du virtuose, l'instrument ne l'intéressait que comme médium sonore. Dans le processus de création, le clavier ne jouait chez Haydn et Mozart qu'un rôle secondaire : ils composaient à leur table de travail (Mozart préférait même composer de tête). Beethoven, en revanche, ne pouvait ni créer ni vivre sans piano. Il improvisait suivant son imagination, pendant des heures, avant de coucher sur le papier ses idées musicales. Le piano lui servait à catalyser la violence de ses sentiments, les touches l'aidaient à donner forme sonore à son âme. Il détestait que des voisins l'épient quand il improvisait. Jouer du piano dans la solitude, c'était pour lui tout en même temps prière, profession de foi et méditation. Beethoven fut un homme très solitaire, tourmenté dès l'âge de trente ans par des troubles de l'audition qui le menèrent en quelques années à une surdité totale. Une catastrophe pour un musicien qui avait dans sa jeunesse un talent de pianiste promis à un magnifique avenir. Il est difficile de s'imaginer Beethoven en favori du public, s'inclinant à maintes reprises devant les auditeurs après avoir joué de manière « charmante » et envoyant des baisers aux dames. C'est pourtant ainsi qu'il commença sa carrière dans sa ville natale, Bonn. Enfant prodige, il fut souvent, sous la férule brutale de son père, impitoyablemeent entraîné pour paraître en public. Qand furent imprimées pour la première fois ses compositions pour piano, on le rajeunit de deux ans sur la page de titre. Lorsque, à l'âge de vingt-deux ans, il alla s'installer à Vienne, il voulait avant tout faire la conquête de l'élégante société de la ville impériale grâce à son jeu de pianiste : il portait un frac vert, prenait en parfait dandy des cours de danse er d'équitation. Le destin en décida autrement, et le jeune musicien à l'avenir tellement prometteur fut peu à peu coupé du monde extérieur. Il resta seul avec son piano.

Le style de Beethoven au piano

Nous paierions cher pour posséder un enregistrement du jeu de Beethoven au piano, ce qui est malheureusement impossible car il vécut des décennies avant l'ère d'Edison. Diverses descriptions nous sont parvenues, évoquant la manière dont les sons déferlaient en tempête sous ses doigts, menaçaient, ou, dans les notes hautes du clavier, scintillaient comme des étoiles. Les partitions en révèlent bien davantage. Elles nous font savoir que Beethoven était un artiste des contrastes. Il aimait les registres extrêmement graves ou aigus, il écrivait parfois des trilles extra-ordinairement longs, indiquait des pauses inattendues et faisait souvent «dialoguer» la main droite et la main gauche. Le style de ses compositions pour piano se modifia au fil du temps. Dans sa jeunesse, il subit l'influence de Mozart et Haydn ; vers 1800, il affirma un nouveau et personnel style avec une grande conscience de soi, et au soir de sa vie, il nota des sons qui n'étaient pas seulement pleins de hardiesse er d'étrangeté, mais que la postérité ne sut jamais imiter, comme s'il s'agissait d'une musique venue d'une autre planète.

L'œuvre pour piano de Beethoven

L'œuvre pour piano de Beethoven est gigantesque. Ses 32 sonates pour piano constituèrent pour des générations de pianistes un programme suffisant pour remplir toute leur vie. Tout ce que l'on savait depuis J. S. Bach sur la musique pour clavier, on le trouve avec une exhaustivité encyclopédique dans les sonates de Beethoven pour piano. Elles forment son «journal» musicale : il écrivit la première à treizel ans, la dernière cinq ans avant sa mort. Toute sa vie, cependant, il pratiqua une autre forme musicale : la variation. Ce sont les variations pour piano qui ont éternisé l'extraordinaire faculté d'improvisation de Beethoven. Il est tout à fait caractéristique que sa première et sa dernière œuvre importantes pour clavier aient été des variations. À cela s'ajoutent 5 concertos pour piano (entre 1795 et 1809) et un grand nombre d'œuvres pour musique de chambre où le piano joue le rôle principal (surtout des sonates pour violon et violoncelle et des trios avec piano). La création de Beethoven est construite selon une logique remarquable, dans laquelle les compositions pour piano jouent un rôle non seulement très important, mais récurrent dans chaque phase de sa vie. En effet, c'est toujours à travers sa musique pour piano que Beethoven a préparé et annoncé l'avènement d'un nouveau style. Quand il eut, sur son piano, ouvert la nouvelle voie pour lui-même, vinrent les symphonies représentatives (neuf en tout, de 1800 à 1824), et les quatuors à cordes, qui résument et distillent musicalement l'ésprit nouveau (six dans le cycle de l'opus 18, 1800 ; 3 *Quatuors Rasumowsky* op. 59 ; deux quatuors isolés op. 74 et 75, 1809–1810, et les cinq derniers quatuors à corde, avec la *Grande Fugue*, entre 1823 et 1826) Cette périodicité révèle que Beethoven a conçu dès le début l'ensemble de ses compositions comme une unité architecturale, œuvre de toute sa vie. Dans ce cosmos, les plus petites pièces pour piano, les diverses danses, bagatelles (parmi lesquelles la célèbre *Lettre à Elise*, composée aussi à l'origine comme une « bagatelle ») trouvent aussi leur place et ont leur importance.

6 deutsche Tänze

WoO 8, No. 1

WoO 8, No. 2

WoO 8, No. 3

Trio

Trio

Da Capo

18

6.

Trio

Da Capo

6 Ecossaises

Dal 𝄋 al 𝄌

Dal 𝄋 al 𝄌

Dal 𝄋 al 𝄌

Dal 𝄋 al 𝄌

6 ländlerische Tänze

5.

6.

Coda

Anglaise in D

Hess 61

Allemande in A

WoO 81

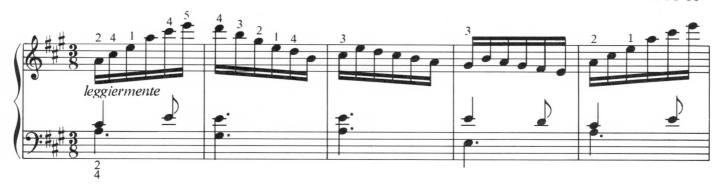

leggiermente

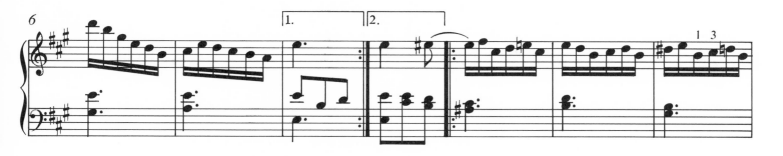

Da Capo

2 Menuette

Trio

Da Capo

Trio

Da Capo

4 deutsche Tänze

WoO 13, No. 6

1.

Trio

Da Capo

30

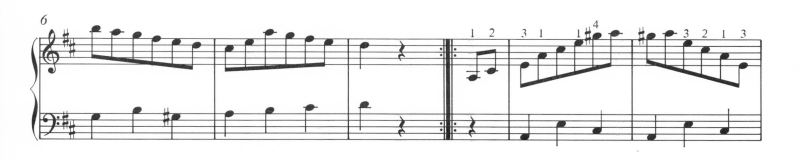

Trio

Da Capo

3.

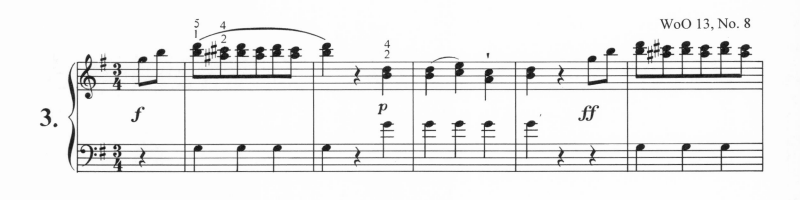

Trio

Da Capo

K 243

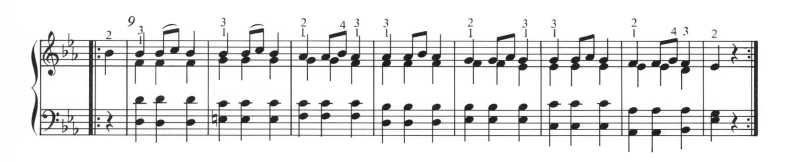

Trio

Da Capo

2 Contredanses

34

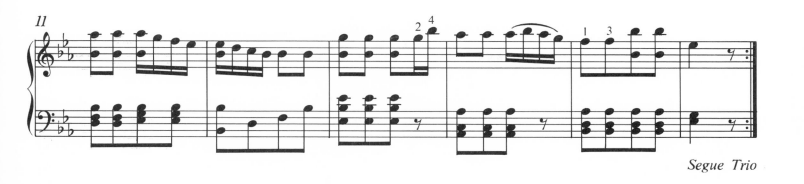

Segue Trio

Trio

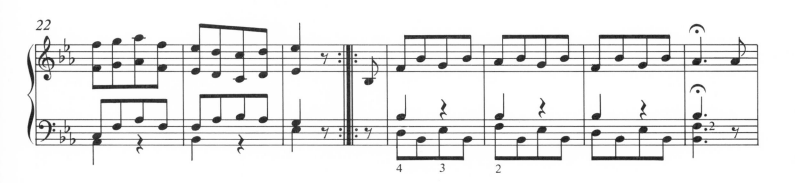

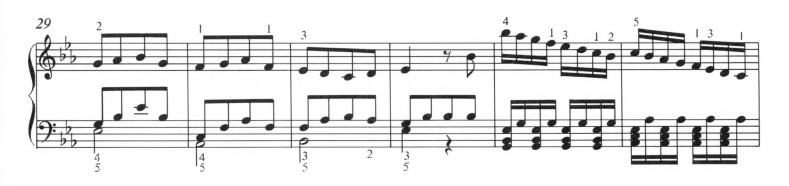

No. 2 Da Capo

2 Walzer

1.

Trio

Da Capo

K 243

2.

Ecossaise in Es

Menuett

Da Capo

2 Sonatinen

Kinsky-Halm Anh. 5

1.

Romanze

K 243

41

2.

Allegro assai

42

K 243

Rondo

Allegro

44

Marcia

Klavierstück
(Lustig-traurig)

il fine

Da Capo

Für Elise

Klavierstück

5 Bagatellen

Allegretto

Op. 119, No. 1

K 243

Andante cantabile

Vivace assai ed un poco sentimentale

Op. 119, No. 9

3.

Allegretto

Op. 33, No. 3

4.

56

60

6 Variationen
über ein Schweizer Lied

Thema

Andante con moto

Var. III Minore

Var. IV Maggiore

Var. V

Var. VI

Coda

K 243

63

6 Variationen
über "Nel cor più non mi sento"

Thema

Var. I

Var. II

66

Var. III

Var. VI

Rondo in A

Allegretto

74

Rondo in C

Allegretto

K 243

Rondo in C

K 243

K 243

K 243

Piano Step by Step

Step by step to the top – this is the idea behind Könemann Music's piano-teaching series. This is not a dogmatic piano tutor but a collection of performance pieces, each selected for a particular didactic purpose and dedicated to a specific problem. Pieces ranging from easy to more demanding are collated in each volume, with each book a complete course of study. Years of experience and practice in piano teaching and lively exchanges of ideas with various piano teachers have helped determine the contents and layout of these books.

The editor of **Piano Step by Step** is *Ágnes Lakos*.

Etüden

This is a collection of classic studies for piano. These mini-compositions by Czerny, Gurlitt, Bertini, Köhler and others are sorted according to various problems of technique. Individual chapters are devoted to playing legato, to chords, dexterity, ornaments, repetition and octaves, among other topics. Each group of études is rounded off with several performance pieces which concentrate on the same technical problems as dealt with in the chapter.

Early Dances

This volume is packed with dances from the Baroque to the Biedermeier period, with composers spanning the spectrum from Bach to Schubert. The layout of this collection is particularly instructive, with the pieces arranged according to types of dance. Whether you'd like to play allemandes, sarabandes, minuets or waltzes, you will find a large selection of examples of each dance form which also adeptly illustrates the differences between dances in various countries and periods.

Introduction to Polyphonic Playing

Polyphony: an important compositional technique and a great technical challenge for the pianist. How is it possible to correctly articulate several different voices at the same time without sacrificing the transparency of each line? To this end, very easy pieces with two or three voices have been put together in this volume, with the stylistic palette ranging from Diruta and Frescobaldi to Reger and Bartók. Two- and three-part Bach inventions printed at the end of each section mark the technical goal of the various chapters.

Sonatinen I
Sonatinen II
Sonatinen III *(In preparation)*

Before we tackle the great sonatas, there are plenty of smaller sonatinas to be enjoyed. The Classical period offers a rich assortment of these compositions which are both technically and musically demanding. Clementi, Kuhlau, Diabelli, Vaňhal and Benda were composers who understood how to produce sonatinas which were not just mere finger exercises but significant pieces of music in their own right. In keeping with his we are printing the sonatinas in cycles as the composers originally intended.

First Concert Pieces I (G. Frescobaldi – C. P. E. Bach)
First Concert Pieces II (J. Haydn – L. van Beethoven)
First Concert Pieces III (R. Schumann – J. Brahms)
First Concert Pieces IV (E. Grieg – W. Lutosławski)

The great moment in the life of every young pianist is his or her first public performance. But what should he or she play? Our *First Concert Pieces* series aims to offer a few answers to this all-important question. The concert pieces are sorted by musical period, and among them there is bound to be at least one which suits your level and capability. Luckily, even the great masters were not afraid to occasionally express themselves in smaller forms and simpler methods. Thus here you can find the Bach or Liszt for you and perform it for the pleasure of yourself and others.

Works for Piano Duet I
Works for Piano Duet II

This used to be the most popular form of music-making in the home; whenever two pianists came together, it went without saying that they sat themselves down at the piano to turn out a few duets. Today, the more common constellation is that of teacher and pupil at the keyboard. We have taken this into account in our collections of duets and have included primo and secondo parts which differ in degrees of technical difficulty – and which are printed underneath each other like a score for practical use. The first volume contains works by Diabelli and Vaňhal, the second by Czerny and André.

Mozart: 44 Piano Pieces
Haydn: 23 Piano Pieces
Beethoven: 47 Piano Pieces

Are you dying to play some Mozart? Or some Haydn? Or Beethoven? Even if you don't feel you're up to their more virtuoso compositions for piano you can still make your wish come true. Our selections have a whole range of easy pieces penned by these immortal Viennese geniuses, including some of their favorite works.

The Baroque Pianist

Two music teachers from Finland, Pekka Vapaavuori and Hannele Hynninen, have conceived this extremely useful album which offers a broad introduction to the world of Baroque music. This colorful collection of piano pieces by composers from Cabezón to Bach and Purcell to Rameau is technically undemanding yet of a high musical quality, thus particularly suited to the young pianist. A detailed written section is a welcome supplement to this volume, offering information for those wanting to learn about the composers, various styles and general characteristics of the Baroque age. There are even tips on how to perform the pieces in keeping with contemporary style. Close study of *The Baroque Pianist* will quickly and efficiently make a genuine Baroque pianist out of any piano pupil. The book is embellished with illustrations by Irmeli Huovinen – some in color – depicting the splendid surroundings in which this music once sounded.

Favourite Piano Studies

This is a series of the one thing pianists dislike most: studies. Many think they are monotonous, boring and unsatisfactory. These examples taken from over a span of two hundred years show, however, that they are an indispensable part of any pianist's training. Könemann Music aims to provide musicians with the best and most useful representatives of this musical genre. First comes the work of the classic étude composer, Czerny, in a quality very close to the Urtext edition. Once you've worked through a few of these volumes, you'll soon notice an improvement in your finger dexterity.

The editor of **Favourite Piano Studies** is *András Kemenes.*

Carl Czerny: 100 Exercises, Op. 139
Carl Czerny: The School of Velocity, Op. 299
Carl Czerny: The Art of Finger Dexterity, I–II
    Op. 740 *(In preparation)*

Czerny's name is almost inseparable from the genre of piano studies. His wide musical output includes a vast number of exercises which Könemann Music aims to print a few selected volumes of. Each volume is a course of training which starts with basic exercises and ends with the utmost virtuosity. Each book deals with a particular area of piano technique.

Piano Step by Step

Schritt für Schritt zu den höchsten Gipfeln des Klavierspiels – dieses Programm wird durch den Titel der klavierpädagogischen Serie von Könemann Music ausgedrückt. Es handelt sich nicht um eine dogmatische Klavierschule. Wir bieten vielmehr Sammlungen von Vortragsstücken, die jedoch mit klarer didaktischer Absicht aufgebaut und jeweils einer speziellen Problematik gewidmet sind. In jedem Band werden Stücke von leicht bis schwer aneinander gereiht, womit jeder Band an sich einen ganzen Lehrgang vertritt. Inhalt und Aufbau werden durch langjährige Erfahrung und Praxis in der Klavierpädagogik sowie in regem Meinungsaustausch unter verschiedenen Klavierlehrern bestimmt.

Die Herausgeberin von **Piano Step by Step** ist *Ágnes Lakos*

Etüden

Klassische Stücke der Etüdenliteratur sind hier versammelt. Die kleinen Kompositionen von Czerny, Gurlitt, Bertini, Köhler und anderen sind nach verschiedenen technischen Problemen geordnet. Einzelne Kapitel werden u.a. dem Legatospiel, dem Akkordspiel, der Geläufigkeit, den Ornamenten, der Repetition und dem Oktavspiel gewidmet. Jede Gruppe wird von einigen Vortragsstücken abgeschlossen, die ebenfalls die gleiche technische Problematik aufweisen.

Alte Tänze

Aus den Epochen vom Barock bis Biedermeier sind in diesem Band Tänze vorhanden. Die Reihe der Komponisten reicht von Bach bis Schubert. Besonders instruktiv ist der Aufbau, bei dem die Stücke nach verschiedenen Tanztypen gruppiert sind. Will man Allemande, Sarabande, Menuett oder Walzer lernen, ist aus jeder Gattung eine große Anzahl von Beispielen zu finden, die auch die Unterschiede nach Ländern und Zeitaltern gut illustrieren.

Einführung in das polyphone Spiel

Polyphonie – ein wichtiges kompositorisches Verfahren und eine große klaviertechnische Herausforderung. Wie kann man mehrere Stimmen gleichzeitig mit unterschiedlicher Artikulation zum Klingen bringen, ohne die Transparenz der Stimmen aufzugeben? Besonders einfache zwei- und dreistimmige Stücke sind hier für diesen Zweck versammelt, wobei das Spektrum der Stilrichtungen von Diruta und Frescobaldi bis Reger und Bartók reicht. Die zwei- und dreistimmigen Inventionen von Bach vertreten jeweils den zu erreichenden technischen Stand der einzelnen Teile.

Sonatinen I
Sonatinen II
Sonatinen III *(In Vorbereitung)*

Der Weg zu den großen Sonaten führt durch die kleinen Sonatinen. Das klassische Zeitalter bietet eine reiche Auswahl von diesen Kompositionen, die weder technisch noch musikalisch als anspruchslos bezeichnet werden dürfen. Clementi, Kuhlau, Diabelli, Vaňhal und Benda – diese Komponisten verstanden es, Sonatinen nicht nur als Übungsstück zu schreiben, sondern als vollgültige, inhaltsreiche Musik. Dieser Auffassung entsprechend drucken wir die Sonatinen in Form von Zyklen ab, die den Intentionen der Komponisten folgen.

Erste Konzertstücke I (G. Frescobaldi – C. P. E. Bach)
Erste Konzertstücke II (J. Haydn – L. van Beethoven)
Erste Konzertstücke III (R. Schumann – J. Brahms)
Erste Konzertstücke IV (E. Grieg – W. Lutosławski)

Der große Moment im Leben eines jeden jungen Klavierspielers ist der erste Auftritt vor Publikum. Was aber soll er spielen? Bei der Beantwortung dieser Frage ist unsere Serie der Ersten Konzertstücke behilflich. Die Vortragsstücke sind nach Epochen geordnet, und unter ihnen kann jeder für die eigenen Fähigkeiten das Richtige finden. Es ist doch gut, daß selbst die größten Meister es nicht scheuten, sich in kleinen Formen und mit einfachen Mitteln auszudrücken. Selbst nach kurzer Zeit kann man also "seinen" Bach oder "seinen" Liszt spielen und zur Freude anderer öffentlich aufführen.

Vierhändige Klaviermusik I
Vierhändige Klaviermusik II

Einst war es die beliebteste Gattung von Hausmusik: Wenn zwei Klavierspieler aufeinandertrafen, war es selbstverständlich, vierhändige Klaviermusik aufzuführen. Heute ergibt es sich öfter, daß Lehrer und Schüler sich zusammen ans Klavier setzen. Dieser Situation wollen unsere Sammlungen Rechnung tragen, indem zwischen Primo und Secondo (die übrigens sehr praktisch in Partiturform untereinander gedruckt sind) oft ein ziemlicher Unterschied in der technischen Schwierigkeit besteht. Im ersten Band finden Sie Werke von Diabelli und Vaňhal, im zweiten von Czerny und André.

Mozart: 44 Piano Pieces

Haydn: 23 Piano Pieces

Beethoven: 47 Piano Pieces

Sie möchten auf jeden Fall Mozart spielen? Oder Haydn? Oder eben Beethoven? Selbst wenn man den größten Klavierkompositionen noch nicht gewachsen ist, kann diesem Wunsch trotzdem entsprochen werden. Unsere Auswahl bietet durchgehend leichte Stücke von den unsterblichen Wiener Klassikern, unter denen jeder sein Lieblingsstück finden kann.

Der Barockpianist

Zwei Musikpädagogen aus Finnland, Pekka Vapaavuori und Hannele Hynninen, haben dieses besonders nutzbringende Album konzipiert, das eine vielseitige Einführung in die Welt der Barockmusik bietet. Die bunte Mischung aus technisch einfachen aber musikalisch hochwertigen Klavierstücken von Cabezón bis Bach und von Purcell bis Rameau eignet sich besonders für den jungen Klavierspieler. Eine willkommene Ergänzung dieses Bandes ist ein reichhaltiger Textteil, in dem alle Interessierten zu den Komponisten, Gattungen und allgemeinen Charakteristiken der Barockzeit Informationen finden können. Es werden sogar Hilfestellungen zum stilsicheren Vortrag der einzelnen Stücke gegeben. Ein Studium "Des Barockpianisten" macht aus dem Klavierschüler schnell und umfassend einen richtigen Barockpianisten. Die – teilweise farbigen – Zeichnungen von Irmeli Huovinen zeigen ergänzend die prächtige Umgebung, in der diese Musik einst erklang.

Favourite Piano Studies

Diese Serie bietet gerade das, was Klavierspieler am wenigsten mögen: Etüden. Nach Meinung vieler sind sie eintönig, langweilig und unbefriedigend. Die Beispiele aus zweihundert Jahren zeigen jedoch: Sie sind unverzichtbare Bestandteile einer Pianistenausbildung. Könemann Music beabsichtigt, die besten und nützlichsten Vertreter dieser Gattung den Musikern in die Hand zu geben. Zunächst die Werke des Etüdenklassikers Carl Czerny. Und diese in einer Qualität, die nah am Urtext liegt. Arbeitet man einige Bände durch, spürt man schon bald die Wirkung an der eigenen "Fingerfertigkeit".

Der Herausgeber der **Favourite Piano Studies** ist *András Kemenes*

Carl Czerny: 100 Übungsstücke, Op. 139

Carl Czerny: Die Schule der Geläufigkeit, Op. 299

Carl Czerny: Kunst der Fingerfertigkeit, I–II Op. 740 *(In Vorbereitung)*

Czernys Name ist mit der Gattung der Etüde eng verknüpft. Sein umfangreiches Werk beinhaltet eine unüberschaubare Menge von Übungen, aus denen Könemann Music einige ausgewählte Bände veröffentlichen will. Ein jeder Band enthält einen ganzen Kurs von den Anfängen bis zur höchsten Virtuosität. Dabei widmet sich jeder Band einem speziellen Problem des Klavierspiels.

Piano Step by Step

Le titre de cette collection, consacrée à l'enseignement du piano et éditée par Könemann Music, exprime parfaitement son objectif – accompagner le débutant pas à pas jusqu'au faîte de la maîtrise du piano. Il ne s'agit pas d'un enseignement dogmatique, bien au contraire. Nous avons rassemblé des partitions en les agençant avec un souci de clarté didactique et en les consacrant dans chaque cas à un problème particulier. Chaque recueil offre des morceaux classés par ordre de difficulté croissante et représente un cours intégral. De longues années d'expérience et de pratique de l'enseignement du piano ainsi qu'un vif échange d'idées entre divers professeurs ont permis d'en déterminer le contenu et la composition.

Ágnes Lakos dirige la collection **Piano Step by Step.**

Etüden

Une sélection de partitions d'études classiques. Les petites compositions de Czerny, Gurlitt, Bertini, Köhler, pour n'en citer que quelques-uns, sont classées selon leur difficulté d'exécution. Des chapitres particuliers sont consacrés notamment au legato, aux accords, à la vélocité, aux fioritures, à la répétition et aux octaves. Chaque catégorie s'achève par quelques morceaux qui posent également les mêmes problèmes.

Danses anciennes

Cet ouvrage présente une sélection de danses qui remonte à l'époque baroque et s'arrête après le Biedermeier. La liste des compositeurs va de Bach à Schubert. La structure du recueil est particulièrement instructive puisque les morceaux sont regroupés selon les divers types de danses. Celui qui désire s'initier à l'allemande, la sarabande, le menuet ou la valse, trouvera un grand nombre d'exemples de chaque genre qui illustrent bien les différences selon les pays et les époques.

Introduction à la musique polyphonique

La polyphonie est une méthode de composition importante qui demande une grande habileté d'exécution au pianiste. Comment superposer plusieurs voix aux articulations différentes, sans renoncer à la transparence des timbres ? Des morceaux à deux ou trois voix choisis pour leur simplicité sont rassemblés ici pour en faire la démonstration. La gamme des orientations stylistiques s'étend de Diruta et Frescobaldi à Reger et Bartók. Les créations à deux ou trois voix de Bach représentent le niveau technique à atteindre dans chaque partie.

Sonatinen I
Sonatinen II
Sonatinen III *(En préparation)*

Pour arriver aux grandes sonates, il faut passer par les petites. L'époque classique nous offre une riche sélection de ces compositions, qui ne sont faciles ni sur le plan musical ni sur le plan technique. Clementi, Kuhlau, Diabelli, Vanhal et Benda – autant de compositeurs qui savaient écrire des sonatines qui ne soient pas uniquement des exercices, mais une musique absolument valable et riche. Respectant cette conception, nous imprimons les sonatines sous formes de cycles qui tiennent compte des intentions des compositeurs.

Premières pièces pour concert I
(G. Frescobaldi – C. Ph. E. Bach)
Premières pièces pour concert II
(J. Haydn – L. van Beethoven)
Premières pièces pour concert III
(R. Schumann – J. Brahms)
Premières pièces pour concert IV
(E. Grieg – W. Lutosławski)

Pour le pianiste débutant, la première représentation en public est un moment inoubliable. Mais que doit-il jouer? Notre collection Premières partitions pour concert l'aidera à résoudre cette question. Les partitions musicales sont classées selon les époques et chacun y trouvera le morceau qui correspond à ses capacités. Par bonheur, les grands maîtres eux-mêmes n'ont pas craint de s'exprimer avec simplicité et en formes réduites. Il est donc possible, même en peu de temps, de connaître « son » Bach ou « son » Liszt sur le bout des doigts, et de le jouer pour le plaisir d'autrui.

Pièces pour piano à 4 mains I
Pièces pour piano à 4 mains II

Autrefois, on appréciait plus que tout ce genre de musique dans les salons : quand un pianiste rencontrait un autre pianiste, ils jouaient du piano à quatre mains pour l'assemblée, cela allait de soi. Aujourd'hui, il arrive souvent que le maître et l'élève s'asseyent ensemble devant le clavier. Nous avons envisagé cette situation dans nos recueils dans la mesure où il existe souvent une différence au niveau de la difficulté d'exécution entre les partitions primo et secundo (imprimées de manière superposée, ce qui est très pratique). Le premier album renferme des œuvres de Diabelli et Vaňhal, le second de Czerny et André.

Mozart : 44 Piano Pieces
Haydn: 23 Piano Pieces
Beethoven: 47 Piano Pieces

Vous désirez absolument jouer du Mozart? Ou peut être du Haydn? Ou éventuellement du Beethoven? Même si vous n'êtes pas encore en mesure d'affronter les grandes compositions pour piano, ce souhait peut être exaucé. Nos sélections comptent une rangée complète écrites par ces génies biennois immortels, comprenant quelques de leurs œuvres préférées.

Le piano baroque

Pekka Vapaavuori et Hannele Hynninen, deux professeurs de musique finnois, ont conçu cet album particulièrement intéressant, qui propose une initiation différenciée à l'univers de la musique baroque. Le pot-pourri de mélodies pour piano – de Cabezón à Bach et de Purcell à Rameau – simples au niveau de l'exécution mais de grande valeur sur le plan musical, est particulièrement destiné au pianiste débutant. Un texte instructif offrant des informations sur les compositeurs, les genres et les caractéristiques générales de l'ère baroque complète l'ouvrage avec bonheur. On y trouve même des conseils pour jouer les morceaux sans enfreindre les règles de style. Une étude du Piano baroque transformera rapidement le pianiste en herbe en un musicien baroque accompli. Les dessins – en partie en couleurs – de Irmeli Huovinen font renaître pour le lecteur les lieux somptueux où cette musique résonnait autrefois.

Etudes favorites pour piano

Cette collection propose ce que les pianistes apprécient le moins : des études. Ils sont nombreux à les trouver monotones, ennuyeuses et insatisfaisantes. Les exemples sélectionnés sur deux siècles de musique montrent cependant que les études sont un élément incontournable de la formation du pianiste. Könemann Music a l'intention de rendre accessible aux musiciens les meilleures et les plus utiles représentantes de ce genre musical. D'abord les études classiques de Carl Czerny, dans une qualité proche du texte original. Le musicien qui a travaillé sur plusieurs recueils verra bientôt s'accroître son aisance et sa dextérité.

András Kemenes dirige la collection **Etudes favorites pour piano**.

Carl Czerny : 100 exercices, Op. 139
Carl Czerny : L'étude de la vélocité, Op. 299
Carl Czerny : L'Art de délier les doigts,
        I–II Op.740 *(En préparation)*

Le nom de Carl Czerny est étroitement lié à la composition musicale qu'est l'étude. Son œuvre vaste comprend une quantité impossible à évaluer d'exercices, et Könemann Music veut en éditer quelques recueils sélectionnés. Chaque ouvrage, consacré à un problème spécifique au piano, est un cours couvrant toutes les étapes, de l'initiation à la maîtrise.

The music text of this edition is based
on the Urtext-edition of Beethoven's complete piano works
published by Könemann Music Budapest
(K 197, 198, 202, 139, edited by István Máriássy)

Cover illustration:
Ludwig van Beethoven – portrait by W. J. Mähler, 1815
Oil on canvas, 60 × 70 cm
Gesellschaft der Musikfreunde Wien
Photo: © Archiv für Kunst und geschichte

K 243

Distributed worldwide by
Könemann Verlagsgesellschaft mbH, Bonner Str. 126.
D-50968 Köln

Responsible co-editor: Tamás Zászkaliczky
Production: Detlev Schaper
Cover design: Peter Feierabend
Technical editor: Dezső Varga

Engraved by Kottamester Bt., Budapest

Printed by Kossuth Printing House Co., Budapest
Printed in Hungary

ISBN 963 9059 53 6